Study Guide to

Ready Player One

by Ernest Cline

by Ray Moore

Acknowledgements:

I am indebted to the work of numerous critics and reviewers. Where I am conscious of having taken an idea or words from a particular author, I have cited the source in the text. Any failure to do so is an omission which I will immediately correct if it is drawn to my attention. I believe that all quotations used fall under the definition of 'fair use.' If I am in error on any quotation, I will immediately make a correction when it is drawn to my attention.

Thanks are due to my wife, Barbara, for reading the manuscript, offering valuable suggestions, and putting the text into the correct formats for publication. Any errors which remain are my own

Ernie Cline, 11 July 2015.
(Attribution: Dominic "Count3D" Dobrzensky. Wikimedia Commons. This file is licensed under the Creative Commons Attribution-Share Alike 2.0 Generic license. My thanks to the photographer.)

Contents

Preface

A Study Guide is an *aid* to the close reading of a text; it is *never a substitute* for reading the text. This novel deserves to be read *reflectively*, and the aim of this guide is to facilitate such a reading.

The study guide questions have *no* answers provided. This is a deliberate choice. I am writing for readers who want to come to *their own conclusions* about this text and not simply to be told what to think about it by someone else. Even 'suggested' answers would limit the *exploration of the text* by readers themselves which is my primary aim.

In the classroom, I found that students frequently came up with answers that I had not even considered, and, not infrequently, that they expressed their ideas better than I could have done. The point of this Guide is to *open up* the text, not to close it down by providing 'ready-made answers.' Teachers do not need their own set of predetermined answers in order effectively to evaluate the responses of their students.

Quotations

Quotation are from the paperback edition of the novel: Cline, Ernest. Ready Player One. New York: Broadway Books, 2011. Print.

Spoiler alert!

If you are reading the novel for the first time, you may wish to go straight to the Study Guide: Questions and Commentary section and come back to the introductory sections later since they do explain everything that happens in the novel, including the ending!

Introduction

Plot Summary

The action is set in the mid-2040s. For decades, the world has been facing an "ongoing energy crisis. Catastrophic climate change. Widespread famine, poverty, and disease. Half a dozen wars" (0001, 1). The Great Recession has destroyed the world's economy, and resources are scarce. The OASIS (Ontologically Anthropocentric Sensory Immersive [simulation]) platform, "a massively multiplayer online game" created by James Halliday and Ogden Morrow in 2012 has "gradually evolved into the globally networked virtual reality most of humanity used on a daily basis" because it provides a safer, more exciting and more fulfilling experience than does the real world (0001, 1).

In 2039, Halliday dies leaving no family or heirs. A video is immediately released on the OASIS in which Halliday announces that he intends to leave his fortune and controlling stock in Gregarious Simulation Systems (which owns the OASIS) to the person who can collect the three keys (Copper, Jade, and Crystal) that are hidden throughout the virtual universe of OASIS and pass through the matching gates to find the secret message that Halliday has encoded there. Halliday's Easter Egg Hunt becomes a sensation, and for many an obsession. Those searching for the Egg are referred to as "gunters" (short for "egg hunters"). They devote themselves almost exclusively to studying Halliday's journal, *Anorak's Almanac*, and 1980s pop culture, convinced that it will help them to locate the clues that will lead to the three keys.

Thirteen-year-old Wade is one of millions of full-time gunters who take up the challenge, but for five years no one makes any progress. Then Wade is the first to find the Copper Key and therefore the first name to appear on The Scoreboard. The novel is Wade's account of his involvement with four other gunters, their competition and cooperation with each other, and their bitter rivalry with Innovative Online Industries (IOI), the world's largest Internet Service Provider, which seeks to take control of the OASIS and exploit it to make massive profits.

With the whole world watching, Wade and the other four gunters wage a virtual battle against IOI, opponents who are willing to commit real murder to get to the prize first. The only way for Wade to survive is to win, but he is increasingly aware that he cannot do this alone. Ironically, his obsessive individual pursuit of Halliday's egg leads him to become involved in the real lives of the four fellow gunters.

Why Read this Book?

Published in 2011, the novel received generally positive reviews and subsequently won several literary awards. A film of the novel is set for release in 2018.

Ready Player One by Ernest Cline

This book might just appeal to young people who would normally rather surf the Web or play computer games than sit down with a book – particularly since there is a website!

Important: Issues with this Book

There is no graphic violence in the novel, though there are two murders and a massive computer simulation battle at the climax. There is no graphic sex. Occasionally the adolescent characters use swear words and profanities that might shock some.

Dramatis Personæ: List of Significant Characters

The Developers of the OASIS

OASIS stands for the Ontologically Anthropocentric Sensory Immersive simulation platform – a massive gaming and educational virtual environment.

James Donovan Halliday (avatar name **Anorak**) "was born on June 12, 1972, in Middletown, Ohio. He was an only child. His father was an alcoholic machine operator and his mother was a bipolar waitress" (0005, 53). Halliday had an emotionally traumatic childhood which made it difficult for him to relate socially with real people (especially women). He may have suffered, to some degree, from Asperger's syndrome or autism. An obsessive by nature, he was deeply immersed in the popular culture if the 1980s, the decade in which he was a teenager. Together with his best friend Ogden Morrow, he founded the video game company Gregarious Games which later became Gregarious Simulation Systems (GSS). Working on his own, Halliday created the OASIS, the largest, multi-player gaming environment ever conceived. Although GSS only charged a quarter for access to the OASIS, the creators made millions selling accessories and became billionaires. Halliday died of cancer, a "sixty-seven-year-old bachelor, with no living relatives … without a single friend. He'd spent the last fifteen years of his life in self-imposed isolation, during which time – if the rumors were to be believed – he'd gone completely insane" (0001, 2). On the day following his death in 2039, a video called *Anorak's Invitation* was released on the OASIS in which he explained that he was leaving his entire fortune (in excess of $240 billion) to the person who could find the Easter egg that he had hidden in the OASIS. Halliday's website offered a free download of his journal, *Anorak's Almanac*.

Ogden Morrow (avatar name the **Great and Powerful Og**) worked closely with Halliday on the development of computer games. However, while Ogden saw gaming as a way to educate young people for the real world, Halliday increasingly became obsessed with living inside his own computer simulations. Thus, following the launch of the OASIS, Ogden became concerned that people were using it to escape reality, so he left GSS and developed educational software with his wife Kira until her sudden death in a car accident. Ogden's relationship with Halliday became more distant, and the two had not communicated for a decade until shortly before Halliday's death, when the latter entrusted Ogden with monitoring the hunt for his fortune. Ogden lives alone in Oregon in a vast mansion and rarely appears in public. Once a year, on his birthday, he throws a lavish party on the OASIS at which he appears in the form of his avatar, the Great and Powerful Og. However, he is able to monitor everyone in the OASIS, since when they initially coded the OASIS, Halliday and he gave themselves "'superuser access to the entire simulation.'" Not only is the Og avatar immortal, but it can "'go pretty much anywhere and do pretty much anything'" including entering private chat rooms without being invited (0033, 312).

Kira Morrow (née **Underwood**) died in a car crash ten years before the start of the story. She had known both Halliday and Morrow when she was a British exchange student at their high school and both of the boys had been in love with her. Unfortunately, Halliday was just not able to pluck up the courage to act on his feelings, and so Kira married Ogden. Ogden tells Wade, "'Even after Kira and I got engaged, I think Jim still harbored some fantasy of stealing her away from me … Kira was the only woman he ever loved'" (0033, 325). It was Kira who gave Halliday the nickname Anorak – a joking reference to his obsession with computers and gaming. Finally, it was his jealousy that made Halliday stop speaking to Ogden until near the end of his life when Kira was dead. Right at the end of the novel, we learn that Halliday used her *Dungeons & Dragons* character name, Leucosia, as his password until his death.

Members of Innovative Online Industries (IOI)

IOI is a multinational corporation is the world's biggest Internet Service Provider which has already "attempted several hostile takeovers of Gregarious Simulation Systems, all of which had failed" (0002, 33). The people who work for IOI are the antagonists in the novel.

Nolan Sorrento is the villain of the story plain and simple. He is the head of IOI's Oology division, which is dedicated to searching for Halliday's Easter egg. In this endeavor, he is completely ruthless being willing to exploit every loophole within the game and to have people murdered in the real world. He plans that IOI will find the Easter egg, use Halliday's money to take over the OASIS, and turn it into a massive for-profit venture. Wade writes that "The moment IOI took it over, the OASIS would cease to be the open-source virtual utopia I'd grown up in. It would become a corporate-run dystopia, an overpriced theme park for wealthy elitists" (0002, 33). Nolan's avatar name is IOI-655321 which is his employee number.

The Sixers are IOI employees in the division named after their six-digit employee numbers that all begin with the number 6. Their avatars all look identical. "Joining the Sixers was a lot like joining the military" (0002, 33).

The High Five

The five highest scoring gunters in the early stages of the search for Halliday's egg.

Wade Owen Watts (aka **Bryce Lynch**, avatar name **Parzival**), the narrator and protagonist, was born on "August twelfth, 2026 [and is therefore eighteen years old at the start of the narrative]. Both parents deceased" (0014, 141). Wade's father was shot dead while looting a store, and his mother, Loretta, died of a drug overdose when he was eleven. During his infancy, Loretta worked for the OASIS as a telemarketer by day and an online sex escort by night, and during these work hours she used the OASIS simulation "as a virtual babysitter" to keep him occupied (0001, 15). Wade would play interactive games and learn fundamental skills within the virtual world, thus beginning his infatuation with technology at a young age. As a result, Wade admits that he "was a painfully shy, awkward kid, with low self-esteem and almost no social skills" (0002, 30). At the start of the novel, Wade is eighteen years old and so he is a member of a "generation [that] had never known a world without the OASIS. To us, it was much more than a game or an entertainment platform. It had been an integral part of our lives as far back as we could remember" (0002, 34). He admits that Aech, whom he only meets online, is his "only friend, not counting Mrs. Gilmore" (0002, 36). He lives with his aunt, whom he dislikes intensely, in one of the "stacks" of mobile homes on the outskirts of Oklahoma City (700 Portland Avenue). In his final year of virtual high school (where his username is **Wade3**), the socially awkward Wade spends most of his time inside the OASIS environment where he searches for clues, plays videogames, listens to music, and watches movies of the 1980s. In the real world, he is an overweight teenager with acne, but his avatar "is taller. And more muscular. And he didn't have any teenage acne" (0002, 28). Actually, Wade is very much like Halliday whom he idolizes, and he immediately becomes obsessed with finding the late James Halliday's Easter egg and inheriting his vast fortune. He calls his avatar Parzival after the Arthurian knight Percival who succeeded in the quest for the Holy Grail. He is the first gunter to find the Copper Key and to open the first of the three gates that will lead to Halliday's hidden message. After the failed IOI attempt to kill him, Wade assumes the alias of **Bryce Lynch**, a 22-year old male with a high credit rating and a Bachelor's degree in Computer Science, in an attempt to fool Sorrento into thinking that Wade Watts is dead.

Aech (pronounced 'H') is Wade's best friend, although they have never met in person. Their avatars communicate and meet exclusively through their avatars in the OASIS, but their close relationship suffers when Wade becomes obsessed with the hunt and romantically attracted to Art3mis another avatar gunter. Aech's avatar is "a tall, broad shouldered Caucasian male with dark hair and brown eyes" (0003, 38), but in reality Aech is Helen Harris, a gay African-American, who grew up in Atlanta, Georgia, and is about the same age as Wade. Helen created a white, male avatar not because she psychologically identifies with either whites or males but because an avatar that conformed with society's stereotype made it easier for her to interact with others in the OASIS.

Art3mis (named after the Greek goddess of the hunt) is a famous female blogger on 1980s pop culture. Wade is a big fan of "Arty's Missives" and is very attracted both by her avatar and by the smart things she writes and does. Art3mis locates the Copper Key first but does not acquire it until after Parzival gives her help. Their virtual relationship becomes complicated by their competition/cooperation in the search for the Easter egg. In reality Art3mis is Samantha Evelyn Cook from Vancouver, British Columbia. She has a port-wine birthmark on her face about which she is very conscious (for which reason it does not appear on her avatar which is otherwise quite a realistic representation), and this explains why she is so hesitant about meeting Wade in person and why she reacts so defensively when he tells her that he loves her having only seen her avatar.

Daito is one of the two Japanese 'brothers' who rise to the top of the scoreboard early in the hunt by working as a team. The two have an uncertain and ambiguous relationship with the other three gunters: Parzival, Aech, and Art3mis. Daito's success in the egg hunt catches the attention of Innovative Online Industries (IOI) and he is murdered. Daito's real name is revealed to have been **Toshiro Yoshiaki**; he was not related to Shoto. After his death, we learn that he was a hikikomori, a Japanese word for someone who is a total recluse. This explains why, when Shoto once asked to meet him in the real world, Daito got very angry, and they did not speak for days. He is one of several characters whose only life is within the OASIS.

Shoto poses as Daito's brother but in reality his name is **Akihide Karatsu**. Following the murder of Daito, he collaborates with Art3mis, Aech and Wade to defeat the efforts of IOI to get to the egg first. He reaches out to Wade to inform him of Daito's murder by IOI agents providing Wade with a simcap (video) of Daito being killed, and a news article falsely describing his death as suicide. Shoto gives Parzival Daito's Beta Capsule, trusting that he will be able to use it when the time is right to exact vengeance on IOI. He joins the four remaining avatars in the final assault on Castle Anorak, but his avatar is killed by Mechagodzilla, a robot piloted by Nolan Sorrento.

Real World People Who Interact with Wade

Aunt Alice is Wade's only living relative, being his mother's sister. After his parents' deaths, she took Wade in but only so that she could get extra food stamps from the government. Aunt Alice lives in a trashy double-wide home in one of the more than five hundred stacks located "west of Oklahima City's decaying skyscraper core" where she rents out rooms to lodgers (0001, 21). She is also a drug addict and her boyfriend, Rick, is always willing to beat Wade.

Mrs. Gilmore lives in the stacks in a trailer below Wade's aunt's trailer. She feeds him, gives him shelter when relations with his Aunt are strained, and he calls her "a sweet old lady in her mid-seventies" (0001, 23). Like Aunt Alice, and many others, she is killed in the explosion that destroys the trailer stack.

Mr. Ciders is Wade3's teacher of Advanced OASIS Studies, a senior-year elective subject, at Public School #1873. Unfortunately for him, Wade3 has superior knowledge of this subject and continually points out errors in the textbook, so Cinders avoids having to call on him in lessons.

Some Other Minor Characters

Todd13 is an obnoxious student who attends Public School #1873. Being rich, he enjoys making fun of Wade3's poverty.

I-r0k "fancied himself an elite gunner, but he was an obnoxious poseur" (0003, 42). He makes a failed blackmail attempt against Aech and Parzival that leads the Sixers to the Copper Key.

Genre

Genre is defined as the class or category into which a work of art can be placed on the basis of its content, forms, technique, etc.

Quest Literature

The novel draws heavily on medieval quest literature. This is evident in Wade's choice of the name Parzival, a version of Sir Percival, the knight in King Arthur's court who searched for the Holy Grail as recorded in *Perceval, Conte du Graal* by the French author Chretien de Troyes writing in the Twelfth Century. Other examples of quest stories include the anonymous *Sir Gawain and the Green Knight* and *The Wife of Bath's Tale* by Geoffrey Chaucer both written in the Fourteenth Century.

The medieval quest involves the protagonist in a difficult journey through unfamiliar, sometimes magical, lands towards a goal or an object. The knight has to overcome many obstacles, natural and supernatural, as a result of which he emerges a changed and better man. *Ready Player One* has many of the elements of the medieval quest tale, most notably: riddles, tests of skill, trial by combat, shape shifting, death and reanimation, and confrontation with wizards. Not only does the protagonist succeed in his quest, he shows himself to be worthy of the love of his lady, the fair Art3mis.

Dystopian Fiction

In 1516, Sir Thomas More published *Utopia* a work which combined fiction and political philosophy. The society of Utopia (an island located in the New World) is described in great detail. Although not all aspects of Utopian society appear to be ideal, the book gave its name to any vision of an ideal society. By extension, any work describing a society which is corrupt and evil is called dystopian. *Gulliver's Travels* by Jonathan Swift (1726) is often cited as the first dystopian novel. All writers of dystopian novels since the mid-twentieth century owe a great debt to *Brave New World* (1936) by Aldous Huxley, *Nineteen Eighty-Four* (1949) by George Orwell, and *Fahrenheit 451* (1953) by Ray Bradbury. The genre has recently gained new popularity in the *Hunger Games* trilogy by Suzanne Collins, the *Divergent* trilogy by Veronica Roth and the *Maze Runner* trilogy by James Dashner.

Most of the action of *Ready Player One* occurs within the virtual world of The OASIS. Nevertheless, a world in chaos and collapse is the wider context in which this action occurs. Cline takes aspects of the world in the first two decades of the twenty-first century (particularly global warming and depleted fossil fuels) to explain a global economic, political and social crisis. The danger seems to come less from a tyrannical government (which is struggling to respond to developments beyond its control) than from exploitative big business which seeks to make massive profits from the already poor. Cline uses this dystopian world as the backcloth for his story, and so the description and analysis of the real world is limited and not always convincing.

Science Fiction

The back cover of the paperback classifies *Ready Player One* as "SCIENCE FICTION," but the novel actually has little of the technological advances we associate with that genre. By launching the OASIS in 2012, "Gregarious Simulation Systems elevated the MMO [massively multiplayer online role-playing games or MMORPGs] to an entirely new level … [with] hundreds (and eventually thousands) of high-resolution 3-D worlds … beautifully rendered in meticulous graphical detail, right down to bugs and blades of grass…" (0005, 57), and it has further developed in the three decades up to the start of the novel. However, aside from the requirement for a massive increase in the processing power of Cloud servers and Internet bandwidth (both hard to reconcile with the economic decline and social disintegration of the world since 2012), the technology is not actually new.

In addition, Wade gives very little explanation of the technological development that has made the OASIS of the mid-2040s possible. We are told that "the OASIS utilized a new kind of fault-tolerant server array that could draw additional processing power from every computer connected to it" and that its success depended on "two pieces of interface hardware that GSs had created, both of which were required to access the simulation: the OASIS visor and haptic gloves" (0005, 58), but that is about as much technical explanation as the reader gets. Though obviously knowledgeable, Cline just does not seem to be interested in the technology which is merely the backcloth for his story. Aside from the OASIS, there is not a single technological or scientific advance described in the novel.

Bildungsroman (The Coming of Age Novel)

A *Bildungsroman* tells the story (often, though not exclusively, in the first person) of the growing up of a young, intelligent, and sensitive person who goes in search of answers to life's questions (including the biggest question of all: who they actually *are*) by gaining experience of the adult world from which they have been hitherto protected by their youth. The novel tells the story of the protagonist's adventures in the world and the inner, psychological turmoil in his/her growth and development as a human being. Examples include: *Great Expectations* and *David Copperfield* by Charles Dickens, *Sons and Lovers* by D. H. Lawrence, *A Portrait of the Artist as a Young Man* by James Joyce, *The Catcher in the Rye* by J. D. Salinger, etc., etc.

Wade's problem is typical of millions of people in the mid-2040s: the real world is such a horrible place that he escapes into the virtual existence of the

OASIS. In Wade's case (as in the case of James Halliday) retreat is motivated also by deep feelings of social inadequacy. However, Wade is placed in a situation that forces him to face up to life. Having known Aech and Art3mis only through their avatars (aware that either of them might be "some middle-aged dude named Chuck" [0002, 35]), the need to win the game necessitates him dealing with them as real people. In addition, his attraction to Art3mis goes beyond her sexy avatar: he wants to meet the real young woman, and he is not disappointed. The final sentence of the novel, "It occurred to me then that for the first time in as long as I could remember, I had absolutely no desire to log back into the OASIS" (0039, 372), suggests the progress he has made. (It will be interesting to see the direction of the promised sequel when it is released.)

Narrative Voice

From the prologue, we learn that the first-person narrator, Wade Watts, is looking back on the events described in the narrative in an attempt to "set the record straight, once and for all" because "[d]ozens of books, cartoons, movies, and miniseries have attempted to tell the story of everything that happened … but every single one of them got it wrong" (0001, 9). It is unclear exactly how many years after his victory he is writing, but he assumes that he is writing for people who are very familiar with the history of the OASIS and who lived through the years of Halliday's egg hunt.

Quite in what sense Wade is setting the record straight is never made clear. As a narrator, he lacks the introspection that would allow him to present his role in the Hunt objectively and the critical faculties to *really* examine the state of the world and the dangerous seductiveness of the OASIS. Wade's narrative is focused purely on telling his story from his own perspective. The reader may wonder just how accurate his version is, but since there is nothing against which to evaluate it, we cannot know.

Ready Player One by Ernest Cline

Setting

The Real World

The action of the novel actually begins in February 2045. For decades the depletion of fossil fuels has caused an "ongoing energy crisis," and global warming has led to, "Catastrophic climate change. Widespread famine, poverty, and disease. Half a dozen wars" (0001, 1). Political and social structures have largely broken down, and the gap between the mega-rich and the mass of the population has grown tremendously. In the USA (and presumably in other countries), the "oil crash and the onset of the energy crisis" meant that cities "were flooded with refugees from surrounding suburban and rural areas" (0001, 21). One attempt to ease the resulting urban housing shortage was to build stacks of trailer homes, at least fifteen high, one on top of one another, held together by a vertical network of girders. Stack collapses are not uncommon, and Wade tells us that "gunfire wasn't uncommon in the stacks" (1.1). The countryside is a dangerous and lawless place which perhaps explains why real food is unavailable (at least to the masses), as we learn when Mrs. Gilmore offers Wade "soy bacon … [and] powdered eggs" (0001.23).

The novel contains no detailed analysis of the socio-economic context in which the action takes place. It is merely presented as a given. Neither Wade nor the author seems to be interested in analyzing its causes and possible solutions. The reader might feel that the world of the novel lacks consistency. How is Aech (a young African-American woman) able to drive her RV all over America when the bus on which Wade travels is armor-plated and guarded? If the countryside is so lawless and depopulated, where does the food come from? If so many people are poor and unemployed, how do they afford OASIS equipment? If the world post-2010 was in an economic decline that seems to have stifled technological advances, how come computing has made such great strides?

Of course, the author could simply respond that his young narrator is not interested in this sort of detail, but the truth seems to be that Cline is much more interested in telling a story that largely takes place within the OASIS than in telling the story of the real world.

The OASIS

The Ontologically Anthropocentric Sensory Immersive Simulation (OASIS) is a virtual reality game and learning environment which is accessed by putting on a visor and haptic gloves and connecting to a main server. (Ontology is a branch of philosophy dealing with the nature of existence, and anthropocentric means that human consciousness is at the centre of this world.) Within the OASIS, it is possible to engage in quests, to play games for money (ironically, its currency [compare bitcoin] is the most stable in the real world),

13

to own artifacts, and to build up credits, but it is also possible to access every book ever written and to attend virtual school where "Teachers could take their students on a virtual field trip every day, without ever leaving the school grounds" (0004, 47). In addition to all of the resources available on the OASIS legally, and at no cost, various illegal sites mean that you can get just about anything else you need – provided you can pay for it.

The quality of the virtual experience varies considerably depending on the hardware the user is able to afford and the speed of their Internet connection. Early in the novel, Wade tells the reader, "I'd heard that if you accessed the simulation with a new state-of-the-art immersion rig, it was almost impossible to tell the OASIS from reality" (0002, 27). Only at the end, when they are guests at the Morrow mansion, do Wade and his friends get to use such state of the art hardware, "'OASIS immersion bays … top-of-the-line Habashaw rigs. OIR-Ninety-four hundreds'" – whatever that is (0033, 324).

The vast majority of the action in *Ready Player One* occurs inside the OASIS since nearly everyone spends most of their time in simulated worlds based on movies, albums, TV shows, and video games from the 1980s as an escape from the grim surroundings of the Earth. The problem is that the OASIS is just too realistic. It "rendered in meticulous graphical detail, right down to bugs and blades of grass, wind and weather patterns" (0005, 57). Wade tells us that "As the era of cheap, abundant energy grew to a close, poverty and unrest began to spread like a virus. Every day, more and more people had reason to seek solace inside Halliday and Morrow's virtual utopia" (0005, 59). The OASIS seems to have replaced religion as "the opium of the masses" (Karl Marx): rather than take control of their lives, they seek an alternative existence, and rather than spending what little money they have on real things, they spend it on virtual stuff to enhance their OASIS experience. It is all pretty sad.

Themes

The novel of ideas is a genre into which *Nineteen Eighty-Four* certainly fits, but *Ready Player One* almost certainly does not. Orwell uses the story (and it is quite a good one) of Winston Smith and Julia in order to dramatize and analyze ideas that he has about the nature of totalitarianism. In contrast, Cline's interest is almost exclusively in plot. As a result, though the novel certainly explores a range of themes these are not usually fully developed. (I should perhaps add that what I have just written is a description of the novel, not necessarily a criticism of it.)

Reality and Virtual Reality

The problem with the OASIS is that it is so realistic that it is hard to tell it from reality. Wade writes that, "I'd come to see my [OASIS] rig for what it was: an elaborate contraption for deceiving my senses, to allow me to live in a world that didn't exist. Each component of my rig was a bar in the cell where I had willingly imprisoned myself" (0019, 198). However, since he says this half way through the book it is clear that he does not act on his epiphany. The OASIS (and particularly the Hunt) is addictive. Cline seems to alternate between criticizing it and celebrating it.

Identity

One of the earliest and best jokes about the Internet was a cartoon by Peter Steiner published by *The New Yorker* on July 5, 1993. A black dog is sitting on a chair in front of a computer saying to another dog sitting on the floor, "On the Internet, nobody knows you're a dog." The same is true of the OASIS which allows a user to select the physical appearance of his/her avatars and through them become anyone he/she wants to be. In the case of the High Five, each one hides his/her true identity to a greater or lesser extent (Helen Harris changes her race, gender and sexual orientation; Toshiro Yoshiaki and Akihide Karatsu present themselves as Samurai warriors; Samantha Evelyn Cook eliminates what she considers her disfiguring birthmark; and Wade Owen Watts trims off a few pounds and gets rid of his teenage acne).

Cline hits most of the prejudices (sexism, racism, homophobia) in his story of the High Five and shows how relatively easy they are to overcome. When Wade finally meets Aech he is shocked, but he soon reflects, "We'd known each other for years, in the most intimate way possible. We'd connected on a purely mental level. I understood her, trusted her, and loved her as a dear friend. None of that had changed, or could be changed by anything as inconsequential as her gender, or skin color, or sexual orientation" (0033, 321). This is the novel's credo: the true nature of friendship. Some readers, however, remain unconvinced. Jarzemsky comments:

It's difficult to determine how we should feel about the characters in *Ready Player One* when they remain so static for the duration of the story. A cynical reader might suspect that Cline, once he neared the end of his manuscript, suddenly remembered that he was writing a book about human beings and hastily threw in a few perfunctory character arcs to keep the audience interested in the ho-hum plot. (John Jarzemsky, "Ready Player One" by Ernest Cline, *Lit Reactor* Review, November 9, 2011)

This is another way of saying that *Ready Player One* is not a novel of ideas. Other themes in the novel are: exploitative capitalism, the value of perseverance, the importance of family (or rather the consequences of the lack of family), the nature of games and competition, and the paradigm shift of a new virtual reality.

Symbolism

Keys, Locks and Gates.

Fundamental to the symbolism of the novel are the three keys which unlock the three gates, but the meaning of these symbols is ambiguous. The three gates are arranged in sequence so that gunters are drawn deeper and more obsessively into the game as they move closer to their goal – Halliday's Easter egg. Up until the time when he finds the first key, Wade maintains some sort of balance in his life. The outside world (hostile and unattractive as it is) still exists for him and even when he is in the OASIS world he goes to high school and accesses a variety of resources. However, from the moment the first gate is opened not only Wade but tens of thousands of gunters become increasingly obsessed by the Hunt. Wade leaves school (from which he has graduated) and spends his entire time on the Hunt. For six months he locks himself in an armor-plated apartment without sunlight in the city of Columbia. He describes his life as a "daily ritual" (0019, 190), using religious language to convey the intensity of his dedication to the game. Yet finally Wade realizes that he has to leave the OASIS and infiltrate IOI, and this forces him to reemerge into the real world. When he finally emerges, he is forcibly struck by what he sees, "A thick film of neglect covered everything in sight. The streets, the buildings, the people ... The number of homeless people seemed to have increased dramatically" (0029, 276). The paradox is that in order to do anything about life in the real world (as Wade, increasingly influenced by Art3mis, wants to do), he has to submerge himself again for the climactic battle that takes place in virtual reality.

Thus, keys, locks and gates are a dual symbol. Wade's journey toward the Easter egg and Halliday's fortune draws him deeper into an existence where the only thing that matters is the Scoreboard, but the process through which Wade goes during his quest also involves him interacting more frequently with real people, forming real friendships and seeing the real world, all of which leads him to conclude that he has "absolutely no desire to log back into the OASIS" (0039, 372). Traditionally keys, locks and gates are sexual symbols (because they carry connotations of penetration). This reminds us that, as in the medieval quest tales, Wade is trying to win the game in order to prove himself worthy of his beloved, Art3mis/ Samantha. Having come to "the grim realization that virtual sex, no matter how realistic, was really nothing but glorified, computer-assisted masturbation" (0019, 193), he dedicates himself to a real love affair. He promises Samantha, "'We can take things as slow as you like'" (0039, 372). It begins with a kiss.

The Egg

The egg traditionally represents birth. On one level, all of the gunters have to *become* Halliday in order to solve the clues, and thus he is figuratively

17

reborn (given a kind of immortality) through them, since they share his passions and obsessions. This process works itself out as Wade immerses himself totally in all things Halliday. However, as we have seen, Wade eventually goes beyond his mentor by turning his back on the OASIS and committing himself to a real-world relationship with Samantha – something Halliday was never able to do with the only woman he ever loved. So the real birth in the story is that of Wade (and to some extent of his three friends), and there is some suggestion that Halliday planned it that way all along since the quest is so designed that it cannot be completed without the gunters working together.

Eggs are, of course, rather fragile. When Halliday gives Wade access to the Big Red Button, he gives him the power to delete that OASIS entirely. Perhaps it has served its purpose. Destroying the OASIS would destroy the virtual economy that generates billions of dollars, but it would force people to rebuild the real economy and thus improve their real quality of life.

The OASIS

The name "the OASIS" suggests a watering place (of culture) surrounded by the desert (of economic and social decline and decay). Put that way, virtual reality sounds quite positive, but the full picture is much more ambiguous. It provides an environment in which everyone has a chance to be successful, regardless of their appearance, race, gender, sexual orientation or nationality, but in the end it is not real success. It is an illusion.

The narrative opens with Wade being "jolted awake by the sound of gunfire in one of the neighboring stacks" and deciding to enter this virtual world where he will play "a few coin-op classics," computer games that are to him "Pillars of the pantheon" that he plays "with a determined sort of reverence" (0001, 13). Thus, the two essential characteristics of the OASIS are immediately established: it is for many an escape from their dreary and dangerous existence in the real world, and it is essentially backward-looking. These tendencies are exacerbated when the Hunt begins because the riddles and clues were written by a man who had become fixated on the pop culture of the 1980s, the decade in which he had been a teenager.

In this aspect, the OASIS symbolizes the sort of 'relief' from reality that is provided by drugs. Art3mis tells Wade, "The OASIS lets you be whoever you want to be. That's why everyone is addicted to it" (0017, 173). Bear in mind that Wade's mother, Loretta, died of a drug overdose when he was eleven and that his Aunt Alice is also a drug addict. Dependency and inability to deal with the real world appear to run in his family. At key moments in the narrative, Wade consciously uses the language of drug dependency to describe his use of the OASIS, but he seems unable to break his addiction. This is, of course, precisely what he does manage to do at the end of the narrative – or perhaps,

Ready Player One by Ernest Cline

like many addicts, he merely thinks he has broken his habit.

Study Guide: Questions and Commentary

The plot drives this novel which makes it a real page-turner. Character development is minimal and settings are sketched in rather than described in full. The questions are designed to be used on your first reading of the story (though they can, of course, still be used if you happen to have read the story already). The aim is not to test you but to help you to understand the text. The questions do not normally have simple answers, nor is there always one answer. Consider a range of possible interpretations – preferably by discussing the questions with others. Disagreement is encouraged! For the reasons stated above, no answers are provided.

The novel is full of references to early computer games and more generally to popular culture in the 1980s. Most of these are either explained in the narrative or do not really need to be explained. For this reason, the notes provided are very selective.

0000 (Preface)

Notes

"the Zapruder film" (2) – a home movie taken by Abraham Zapruder that shows the assassination of John F. Kennedy in Dallas on Friday, November 22, 1963 at 12:30 p.m. Central Standard Time.

"placed in escrow" (4) – placed in a trust and administered by a third party until specific conditions are met.

"'Easter egg'" (5) – a message or other feature hidden by the author(s) within a computer program or game – the first example was, in fact, the hidden message in the Atari video game *Adventure*.

Questions

1. What evidence do you find in the preface that the world of the 2030s and 2040s is dominated by both natural and man-made disasters and that the government employs the media as a means of distracting the people from the realities of existence?

2. Does the preface celebrate or criticize the idea of people being immersed in the virtual world of the OASIS?

Commentary

The world of the novel is a projection of the world as it was in 2011 when it was written. Having failed to switch from fossil fuels, these are almost exhausted, and the problem of global warming caused by carbon emissions has become acute. The result has been increased conflict between nations, widespread famines and disease, and a breakdown of law and order within the U.S.A. In this environment, the government uses the virtual world of the OASIS as a way to distract and manipulate the population.

Halliday is presented as a sad and lonely man unable to cope with the real world who created his own virtual world within the OASIS – the name suggests a refuge from the arid desert. Wade also seems well on the way to becoming an obsessive recluse, almost a clone of Halliday by whom he seems fascinated.

Level One

0001

Notes

"Pillars of the pantheon" (23) – a pantheon is a Greek or Roman temple dedicated to all of the gods – *the* Pantheon is a circular temple in Rome, completed around AD 125.

Questions

3. Explain what the stacks are. What socio-economic change led the authorities to build them? What practical problems and potential dangers are posed to those who live in the stacks?

4. The narrator is the adult Wade, not the eighteen-year-old whose story he tells. This allows the narrator the benefit of hindsight and a mature perspective on what began in 2045. Give one example of the narrator's ability to place his own experience in context in ways that he was not able to do at the time.

Commentary

Wade captures the seductive attraction of video gaming when he writes, "There, inside the game's two-dimensional universe, life was simple: *It's just you against the machine*" (14). He similarly admits to having become "addicted" to watching *Family Ties* which is pure escapism from his own home life. The OASIS is a paradox: it is the ultimate gaming environment, but it is also the ultimate self-educational environment. Wade uses it to discover the truth about the human condition, that "he's been born into a world in chaos, pain, and poverty just in time to watch everything fall to pieces," and to escape from that truth, "OASIS … was like having an escape hatch into a better reality … a magical place where anything was possible" (18). (This dichotomy in the OASIS perhaps reflects the very different personalities, aims and interests of its developers Halliday and Morrow.)

The Hunt rescues Wade from a meaningless existence by providing him with "something worth doing" (19). Given the odds against success, this is a questionable judgment, but given the harshness of his life it is clear why Wade is looking for an escape from reality. Wade is scornful of Mrs. Gilmore's religious faith since he believes that "organized religion was a total crock." However, he is honest enough, in retrospect, to write, "It was a pleasant fantasy that gave her [Mrs. Gilmore] hope and kept her going – exactly what the Hunt was for me" (23). Here Wade shows a maturity of judgment that he was not capable of at age eighteen.

Wade's physical hideout, the van, is his "refuge" from the real world – a place where he can "access the OASIS in peace" and "privacy." He clearly attends a virtual school, reads digital books, watches television shows and movies (mainly from the 1980s), and takes part in the many multi-player games on OASIS. In fact, the only thing he does not do is interact with real people, of whom he seems to know very few.

0002

Notes

"Princess Leia" (27) – Princess Leia Organa of Alderaan (later General Leia Organa) is a fictional character in the *Star Wars* series of movies played by actor Carrie Fisher.

"Monty Python ... *Holy Grail*" (27) – *Monty Python's Flying Circus* was a comedy series broadcast by the BBC between 1969 and 1974 – the group also made five movies between 1971 and 1983 of which *Monty Python and the Holy Grail* (1975) was the second.

"*Time* magazine cover" (27) – *Time* magazine is the premiere news weekly in the U.S.A. – to appear on the cover is high recognition.

"'MacGuffin Hunt'" (35) – a movie term for the object that drives the plot forward because it motivates both the heroes and villains – a treasure map would be an example.

Questions

5. Make an annotated list of the groups and significant individuals who are searching for Halliday's Easter egg. Who are they and what is their motivation?

6. What is it about Art3mis that attracts Wade?

Commentary

The OASIS is a virtual environment in which, with the best equipment, "it was almost impossible to tell the OASIS from reality" (0002, 27). This is, of course, a statement about the sensory experience delivered by the system; the *nature* of that experience is much more enjoyable in the OASIS than it is in the real world. The chapter raises the issue of identity on the OASIS, since a person can make his/her avatar anything they want it to be (except at school where certain rules apply). You can really know nothing about a person from their avatar. Nevertheless, Wade admits to having ""a massive cyber crush on Art3mis" (35). A close reading of his description of Art3mis shows, however, that he is attracted to things about her that would be hard to fake, for example her brilliant writing style and her unorthodox avatar image.

The OASIS is not just a virtual world; it is a virtual universe. Wade's school is located on the planet Ludus, though he lives on earth. The catch is that all avatars are initially placed on the planet Incipio and to move around the virtual universe "you had to pay a teleportation fare ... and that cost money" (31). Also expensive are items the avatar might want to use in the virtual world. This is how the OASIS makes money. Where the majority of the users get this money (other than the virtual currency that they can earn or win) is never made really clear.

0003

Notes

"And don't call me Shirley" (40) – a repeated laugh-line in the 1980 comedy movie *Airplane!*

"*Dragon* magazine" (37) – one of two magazines dedicated to the role-playing game *Dungeons & Dragons* (*Dungeon* was the other)

Question

7. Explain the history and nature of Wade's association with Aech.

Commentary

The chapter introduces a few more characters from Wade's OASIS world, though only Aech will be really important to the story. We also learn how it is possible for people to earn credits (money) and raise the levels of their avatars by earning XPs (experience points): the OASIS offers a vast number of games and competitions.

Wade and Aech have in common their encyclopedic knowledge of 1980s culture, and though I-r0k is a pretty obnoxious character, he has a fair point when he says that they "'both need to get a life'" (45).

0004

Question

8. What are the factors that limit Wade's ability to navigate OASIS?

Commentary

This chapter gives a lot more information on how the OASIS became the biggest virtual environment ever. Although gamers and gunters are the focus of the story, Wade informs us that they are a tiny minority of those who use the OASIS. Most people "only used the OASIS for entertainment, business, shopping, and hanging out with their friends" (50). For people like Wade, however, the OASIS has become an all-consuming addiction that has virtually eliminated their real lives. As in the real world, avatars need money and possessions to do what they want to do, whether that is to travel between worlds or to engage in a PvP contest. Wade's problem is that he is dirt-poor in both the real world and the virtual world.

0005

Notes

"Gygax, Garriott, and Gates" (52) – Ernest Gary Gygax (1938–2008), Richard Garriott de Cayeux (born 1961) and William Henry Gates III (born 1955) each contributed to computer and/or computer game development.

"Jobs and Wozniak or Lennon and McCartney" (53) – Steven Paul Jobs (1955–2011) and Stephen Wozniak (born 1950) co-founders of Apple; John Lennon (1940–1980) and Paul McCartney (born 1942) were original members of the phenomenally successful pop group The Beatles.

"Asperger's syndrome" (55) – the term describes a brain development disorder that leads to problems with social skills, behavior, and coordination – conditions vary in severity – one symptom is that sufferers tend to have an obsessive focus on one topic or to perform the same behaviors again and again.

Question

9. Explain how the success of OASIS was the result both of its technical innovation and the state of society at the time of its launch.

Commentary

Halliday and Morrow were both expert programmers with a passion for computer games. In every other way, they were entirely different personalities. Morrow was good with people and management, so he took control of the business side of the operation; Halliday, "hyperkinetic, aloof, and ... socially inept," was obsessive about game development, so he "locked himself in his office, where he programmed incessantly, often going without food, sleep, or human contact for days or even weeks" (55). The word 'gregarious' (sociable, fond of company) in the names of their two companies seems strange since computer games, and particularly the OASIS, provide an alternative to the real world. The danger is that the "lines of distinction between a person's real identity and that of their avatar began to blur ... [as] most of the human race now spent all of their free time inside a videogame" (60). One can imagine Halliday finding nothing at all wrong with this, but Morrow not being at all happy with it.

Morrow's business model for the OASIS was a very sound one: charge users only a quarter for life-time use, but sell them virtual stuff (clothing, weapons, artifacts, etc.) that costs almost nothing to produce. The two were also able to sell virtual real estate to commercial firms. The result was that Halliday and Morrow quickly became multi-millionaires, but while Morrow used his wealth to see the world, Halliday simply accumulated things.

0006

Question

10. How does Wade find his first clue? Explain its significance.

Commentary

With the benefit of hindsight, Wade describes his obsession with learning about everything in which Halliday had been interested. He admits, "I may, in fact, have started to go a little insane" (62), and that, "I was obsessed. I wouldn't quit. Mt grades suffered. I didn't care" (63). Looking back, he reflects, "You'd be amazed how much research you can get done when you have no life whatsoever" (64). To state the obvious, the narrator must subsequently have 'got a life' in order to make a comparative comment. This foreshadows the ending of the novel.

0007

Notes

"warez sites" (71) – sites offering illegally copied software.

"Doctor Who's TARDIS" (73) – the *Doctor Who* series began on the BBC on Saturday, November 23, 1963 – the Doctor travels in both time and space in a Time And Relative Dimension In Space (TARDIS) machine which has, by an irreversible malfunction, taken on the permanent form of a blue, 1960's British police telephone box.

Questions

11. Explain how Wade deduces the location of the Tomb of Horrors. What seems so logical to him about the answer he discovers?

12. How does Wade's involvement in the Hunt impact his friendship with Aech?

Commentary

Halliday's dedication to education is stressed. Before he died he "set up a foundation to ensure that the OASIS public school system would always have the money it needed to operate" (69), and Wade comes to the conclusion that the Copper Key was hidden on Ludus because Halliday "wanted a schoolkid to find it" (70).

Aech is Wade's best, and only, friend, even though they only meet in the virtual world. However, Wade is determined to find Halliday's Easter egg all by himself. Thus, when Wade needs transportation, he rejects the idea of asking Aech for a loan partly because he would have to lie to him, but also because "any excuse I gave would make him suspicious" (72). Similarly, Wade does not respond to Aech's call because live video would reveal his location and audio-only "might make him suspicious" (74). The Hunt seems to be further isolating Wade and making him a complete loner.

0008

Question

13. Explain how Wade knows where to find the door that the Copper Key will open.

Commentary

As in much of the novel, the emphasis in this chapter is on action: the author recreates the gaming experience in the reader's imagination. One other point is stressed: Wade only succeeds in defeating Acererak/Anorak at *Joust* because he has played the game a lot with Aech, honing his skills until he "got good enough to beat Aech, repeatedly and consistently" (81). This seems to indicate that the Hunt is not an individual enterprise but a joint venture – a lesson that Wade will eventually learn.

The sudden appearance of an avatar at the end of the chapter highlights the author's use of another narrative device: the hook. As you read the novel you will notice how often chapters end with an unexpected twist or on a 'cliff-hanger' in order to make the reader want to read on.

0009

Notes
"Howard Jones" (91) – John Howard Jones (born 1955) is an English musician, singer, and songwriter who had many hit singles and albums between 1983 and 1986.

"Rain Man" (95) – in the 1988 movie of that title, Dustin Hoffman plays the part of Raymond, an autistic savant.

"'Chaotic Neutral'" (96) – a category of characters in *Dungeons & Dragons* – freedom-loving characters who follow their own instincts rather than societies rules, ethics, and traditions.

Question
14. Compare and contrast the characters and motivations of Wade and Art3mis.

Commentary
Art3mis is very different from Wade: she is communicative where he is introverted. It is Art3mis who suggests that they can "'alternate days until one of us beats [Acererak/Anorak]'" (90), and she is the one who does most of the talking because she's been "'dying to talk to someone about all of this'" (92). Her influence wins Wade over: the two show each other mutual respect and rise about the usual trash talk in which avatars engage. Even after Art3mis discovers that Wade has lied to her about not having found the Copper Key, she still offers him valuable advice about the danger he is now in because people know that his avatar has found the first key (something Wade has not thought of). She tells him, "There are a lot of people who would kill for that information" (97). The key question that their meeting poses is: Can competitors still be friends?

The difference between the characters of the two friends is reflected in their plans to use Halliday's fortune should they win it. Wade wants to blast himself into space in a biosphere to escape Earth's problems, while Art3mis wants to "'make sure everyone on the planet has enough to eat ... tackle world hunger ... [and] figure out how to fix the environment and solve the energy crisis'" (98). Both visions are ultimately naïve, but one is essentially selfish and the other altruistic.

[At one point, Art3mis says, "'Chaotic Neutral sugar'" (96). This is a *huge* clue to her real-world identity.]

0010

Notes
"John Cougar Mellencamp" (102) – (born 1951) is an American musician, singer-songwriter, painter, and actor.

Question

15. Identify the two main threats to Wade at present.

Commentary

Lots more gaming plot in this chapter. The "trash" from the riddle is a slang term for the primitive TRS-80 computer, of which Wade finds a replica in Halliday's bedroom. He loads a copy of the game *Dungeons of Daggorath* and having beaten this game-within-a-game, the first gate appears inside a movie poster of *WarGames*.

Once again, the distance between Wade and Aech is growing. Wade has been in "a null-communications zone" (100) for hours, but even when he emerges the Hunt takes priority so Wade sends "him a short text message, promising to call as soon as I could" (100). Two factors seem to be operating on Wade: his intense competition with Art3mis and his strong attraction to her.

0011

Notes

"NORAD ... ICBMS" (112) – North American Aerospace Defense Command ... Inter Continental Ballistic Missiles.

Question

16. Explain how Wade gets through the First Gate.

Commentary

Wade's closing dream is ominous: it reminds us that whilst avatars that die in the OASIS can be replaced by their player, in the real world people who die do so permanently. What is a game in the OASIS is for real in the world: winning the game means getting a fortune, and to achieve that, people are prepared to be completely ruthless. Art3mis and Aech are not Wade's most threatening rivals.

0012

Question

17. Wade writes, "I'd always suspected that Morrow knew more about the contest that he was letting on." What evidence is given that might support this conclusion?

Commentary

More backstory. Halliday and Morrow had very different personalities, the latter having "a much greater connection to humanity. And a great deal more tragedy" – if you think about it, those two things tend to go together (119). It does not take a genius to work out that Kira had something to do with the split between Halliday and Morrow, but there were also fundamental disagreements about the function of computer games. Morrow came to feel that OASIS "'had become a self-imposed prison for humanity ... A pleasant place for the world to hide from its problems while human civilization slowly collapses ...'" Morrow and Kira believed that computer games should teach players the skills necessary to live in the real world not be a refuge from it, and so they "started a non-profit educational software company" (120). Morrow is united with Halliday, however, in not wanting OASIS to fall into the hands of IOI which he calls "'a fascist multinational conglomeration'" (118).

When he finally does contact Aech, Wade does give him some helpful advice, though he wonders if he will come to regret it. Wade is learning the value of cooperation.

0013

Question

18. Why does Wade not follow his "first impulse ... to delete every single copy of the email [from the Sixers of IOI] and pretend [he'd] never received it" (133)?

Commentary

Up to this point, the novel has lacked an antagonist. It is true that everyone involved in the Hunt is in competition with everyone else, but Wade is only in contact with Aech and Art3mis and his relationship with them, though ambiguous, is not really antagonistic. Enter the 'bad guys' of IOI – the corporate villains who represent everything that both Halliday and Morrow hated.

0014

Notes

"cojones" (138) – literally: balls (or testicles) – figuratively: courage.

Question

19. Why is Wade so shocked that the Sixers have actually blown up the stack?

Commentary

Wade's interview with Sorrento leaves the reader in no doubt who the villain is. So far the action of the novel has been played out in a virtual world where avatars die but players can get new avatars. In this chapter, the action reverts to the real world in which people who die disappear forever. This reminds the reader that the stakes of the Hunt are really high. Wade underestimates Sorrento: he cannot believe that IOI will actually kill in order to win the Hunt. However, at least temporarily, Wade has an advantage over Sorrento because IOI is convinced that he is dead.

0015

Question

20. What are the possible explanations for the "stack of comic books on the other side of the room" suddenly sliding off the end table and crashing to the

floor (158)?

Commentary

The chapter explores the ambiguous and unstable relationship of the High Fives: ultimately each one is a solo gunter (with the possible exception of the two brothers. They are completely outgunned (literally) by the Sixers, but still unwilling to give up their independence. Probably the greatest single advantage that the Sixers have is the ability to switch control of their avatars from one operator to another. This means that they always have the most qualified player to meet every challenge, riddle and combat. This is, of course, counter to the values of the Egg Hunt, but it is not technically against the rules because, as Sorrento explains to Wade, "'Halliday's contest doesn't have any rules. That's one of the collosal mistakes the old fool made'" (0014, 138).

At the end of the chapter there is another of those hooks that the author uses so effectively. Fairly obviously, the comic books do not fall as a result of "'a software glitch or something'" (158). They fall over because someone, or something, knocks them over. So what are the possibilities?

0016

Question

21. What further information does the reader obtain about the conditions in the real world in which the action is set?

Commentary

In this chapter, the reader gets another glimpse of the perilous state of the real world. Populations have moved to the cities and the countryside has become a lawless place. The bus in which Wade travels from Oklahoma City to Columbus, Ohio, is a "rolling fortress" with "six heavily armed guards" and "armor plating [with] bulletproof windows" (163). Wade notes that "the view was perpetually bleak, and each decaying, overcrowded city we rolled through looked just like the last" (165). With high unemployment and relatively low wages, corruption is rife. Understandably, Wade decides to "abandon the real world altogether until I found the egg" (166). Check out, however, the epigram under the title "Level Two" and note the contrast.

Level Two

0017

Notes

"Clouseau" (170) – Inspector Jacques Clouseau the bumbling detective in *The Pink Panther* series, played most memorably by Peter Sellers.

"Dr. Lecter" (172) – Dr. Hannibal Lecter the insane serial killer in a series of suspense novels by Thomas Harris (later made into movies).

"John Draper" (176) – John Thomas Draper (born 1943) computer programmer and hacker.

Questions

22. What progress does Wade make on the second riddle?

23. What are the inherent dangers of Wade's developing relationship with Art3mis?

Commentary

Having got the perfect situation to pursue the Hunt 24/7, Wade allows himself to be distracted – or perhaps it is a sign that he wants to live in the real world after all. His attraction to Art3mis appears to be returned, at least when they are communicating in the virtual world. Two obstacles that stand in their way are the Hunt, in which they are rivals, and Art3mis's obvious reluctance to give anything away about her actual appearance.

0018

Notes

"Max Rockatansky" (182) – title character and protagonist in the *Mad Max* films.

"Connor MacLeod" (184) – the protagonist of the Highlander films.

Question

24. Why do you think that Art3mis reacts the way she does when Wade confesses that he is in love with her? Who is right, Wade or Art3mis?

Commentary

At least on the face of it, Wade and Art3mis have different values. Wade has finally found something that he wants more than he wants anything in the virtual OASIS world, including the wealth and fame of finding the egg, but Art3mis is more dedicated to the Hunt than to anything else because of the good that she can do with the prize money. On a deeper level, however, Art3mis's reaction is about her deep uncertainty that Wade will love the person she really is. When she insists, "'Trust me. If I ever let you see me in person, you would be repulsed ... I'm hideously deformed...'" (186), the passion with which she speaks convinces the reader that this is her real reason for breaking off with Wade. Take a look at the final sentence of the chapter and you will be convinced.

The Sixer attack is designed to kill Parcival and Art3mis. Of course, Wade and the girl would be able to take on new avatars, but they would have lost all of their powers and literally be starting again from level one.

0019
Question
25. "I was just another sad, lost, lonely soul, wasting his life on a glorified videogame" (198). How accurate is Wade's description of himself?

Commentary
There is a detailed description of the ultra-sophisticated equipment that Wade has installed. Following the split with Art3mis, he has entirely cut himself off from the real world which seems inferior to the world of the OASIS, "The real world looked washed-out and blurry by comparison" (192). Wade tells us, "The hour or so after I woke up was my least favorite part of the day, because I spent it in the real world. This was when I dealt with the tedious business of cleaning and exercising my physical body. I hated this part of the day because everything about it contradicted my other life. My real life, inside the OASIS" (195). Rather like Art3mis, Wade feels his real self to be inadequate, "an antisocial hermit. A recluse … with no real friends, family, or genuine human contact" whereas on the OASIS he is the "World-famous gunter and international celebrity" (198). Ironically, Wade is in the best physical shape of his life.

0020
Question
26. Explain the reasons why both Wade's life and his quest, appear to have stagnated.

Commentary
This is another chapter in which the plot seems to tread water. Wade has become even more isolated because, having been dumped by Art3mis, he has been unable to renew his previous friendship with Aech, "We'd grown apart, and I knew it was my fault" (203). Wade's stronghold on Falco, his own private planetoid, is an apt symbol for his increasing isolation.

Wade does, however, re-establish good relations with Daito and Shoto which whom he wins the Beta Capsule which allows "the avatar who possessed it to transform into Ultraman once a day, for up to three minutes" (205). (Spoiler alert! This will be of crucial significance in the climax of the novel.)

Wade is also working forty hours a week as a Happy Helpdesk representative. He hates this job and one wonders how he has any time or energy to keep working on the latest riddle. Art3mis clearly has no such distractions because, in another effective hook, we learn in the final sentence that she has found the Jade Key.

0021

Notes

"The Vonnegut … [named] after one of my favorite twentieth-century novelists" (213-214) - Kurt Vonnegut, Jr. (1922 – 2007) amazingly productive American novelist – if you have not read *Slaughterhouse-Five* (1969) you really must.

Question

27. What factors reenergize Wade to search for the Jade Key?

Commentary

This chapter is a jumbled mixed bag of past and present – deliberately so, the reader assumes since it gives the impression that the pace of the narrative is really picking up. Two artifacts are described: the Catalyst, which when detonated "would kill every single avatar and NPC in the sector, including its owner," (209), and Fyndoro's Tablet of Finding, which allowed the user, once a day, to "write any avatar's name on its surface, and the tablet would display that avatar's location at that exact moment" (209). Since both artifacts are in the hands of the Sixers, this foreshadows their use at crucial times in the Hunt.

0022

Question

28. Having played a perfect game of Pac-Man, Wade wins a quarter that seems to be of no value at all since he cannot even take it out of his inventory once he has put it in. Speculate on its significance.

Commentary

The description of the Pac-Man game will appeal to readers who are into computer games. What seems to be a dead end is not: that quarter will obviously prove to be important, and Aech's tip gets Wade back on track.

0023

Question

29. Explain how Wade's knowledge of the early text adventure game Zork should have alerted him sooner to the solution of the second quatrain.

Commentary

At least Wade acknowledges Aech's help in getting to the Jade Key. Actually, he goes further by admitting "to being a colossally insensitive, self-centered asshole" and begging Aech to forgive him (232). This self-knowledge seems to have come too late to rebuild bridges with his ex-best friend. More worrying is that "Daito had just been killed" (233). Of course, "Daito" is just an avatar. Right?

0024

Question

30. How would you account for the sudden success of the Sixers?

Commentary

Things are spinning out of Wade's control as the Sixers discover the third key. In a moment of epiphany, Wade writes, "You know you've totally screwed up your life when your whole world turns shit and the only person you have to talk to is your system agent software" (237). More importantly, "Daito" (or more accurately the person who operated the Daito avatar) is dead.

0025

Question

31. Explain the difference between the Sixers killing Daito's avatar and them killing Daito.

Commentary

The item Daito willed to Parzival is Daito/Yoshiaki's Beta Capsule, the artifact that allows its user to transform into Ultraman. Since this chapter contains a graphic description of Daito's powers as Ultraman there will be no need to explain when (as is clearly foreshadowed) Wade uses the Beta Capsule.

The Sixers kill Yoshiaki just as they tried to kill Wade and they do so in a way that avoids suspicion. In the case of Yoshiaki's death, the Japanese newsfeed article (I am reminded of the telescreens in 1984 by George Orwell) explains it as "ANOTHER OTAKU SUICIDE … Toshiro Yoshiaki, age twenty-two, had jumped to his death from his apartment" (242).The High Five are now the fragmented Four, but at least Shoto and Wade seem to have come together and to have redoubled their determination to win the Hunt.

0026

Question

32. Explain how the square piece of foil in which the Jade Key was wrapped provided Wade with the clue to the location of the Crystal Key.

Commentary

This chapter is full of exciting action first in a virtual replica of the Tyrell Building (from *Blade Runner* the 1982 American science fiction film directed by Ridley Scott) and then inside a 3-D version of Black Tiger. A reader familiar with computer games is probably able to visualize the action better than the rest of us. The prize for winning Black Tiger is a choice from a range of giant robots all from the films, comics and novels of the 1980s. Of course, since lots of gunters have already reached this stage, some of the best ones have gone, but Wade seems more than happy with his choice of Leopardon, Spider-Man's gigantic robot. This prize foreshadows a climax in which the gunters' robots battle one another.

0027

Question

33. Explain how the Sixers learn that Halliday's egg is "located somewhere on the planet Chthonia, inside Castle Anorak" (265).

Commentary

Unlike the earlier stages of solving the clues of the Hunt, having got through the second gate, Wade knows exactly where to find the Crystal Key. The clue is the glowing red star which points to the album *2112* by Rush. Depending on the reader's own interests, the detailed description of how Wade locates and secures the Crystal Key will either be fascinating or tedious (or somewhere between the two). Nevertheless, the chapter ends on a high point of excitement since the Sixers appear to have Castle Anorak completely secured, but Wade has a cunning plan that has a good chance of getting him killed. The important thing is that he knows that he will need to work with the other three (Art3mis, Aech and Shoto) so he sends them the information about how to find the Crystal Key. He has learned that working on his own is not enough, and perhaps that is the point of Halliday's Egg Hunt.

LEVEL THREE

0028

Question

34. What exactly are the IOI corporate police? Explain what is meant by "doing a C-section" (270).

Commentary

The actions shifts to the real world. Wade tells us, "they led me outside, and sunlight hit my face for the first time in over half a year" (274). Actually, the description of the IOI police breaking into Wade's apartment sounds like something out of a computer game. The reader assumes that the charges of debt against "Mr. Lynch" are fabricated, but be cautious: Wade seems to be waiting for the IOI police. They intend to place him in "'mandatory indenture'" until he has paid his debt to the company in full. Note the unconscious irony of Michael Wilson's statement that Lynch is "'now eligible for mandatory indenture,'" which is an oxymoron (270).That means that he will work for the company until his wages have eliminated his debt, something that you can bet would never happen. Bear in mind that IOI does not know that Wade is Bryce Lynch and so that Mr. Lynch is Parzival.

0029

Notes

"*THX 1138*" (277) – a 1971 movie directed by George Lucas set in a 25th-century totalitarian state where mankind is totally controlled by android police and the mandatory taking of drugs to suppress emotion.

Question

35. Wade tells the reader, "I had a plan, and this [i.e., becoming an indentured worker for IOI] was part of it" (278). Later, Wade calls his plan an "idiotic risk to win over someone [Art3mis] I'd never actually met" (282). What do you think Wade has in mind?

Commentary

Amazingly, living conditions in the real world have worsened in the six months Wade has remained in his apartment. Poverty, unemployment and homelessness seem to be endemic. No wonder OASIS is a "far more pleasant reality" in which even the poorest seem to spend most of their lives.

Life for the indents inside IOI Headquarters seems to be similar to that of the Outer Party members in George Orwell's *1984* – except that the technology has improved. Indents are controlled by a combination of propaganda, surveillance and coercion. Evidently Wade's plan involves infiltrating the IOI organization, but even to Wade than plan seems "completely insane" (282). One positive aspect is that Wade's aim is no longer to win the Hunt and the resulting fortune: he wants the Hunt to be over (so long as IOI does not win) so that he can meet Art3mis.

0030

Questions

36. List the reasons why becoming an IOI employee is out of the question for Wade.

37. What happens to change Wade's initial plan? What parts of the initial plan now become obstacles?

Commentary

Wade explains his plan. What we the reader did not know was that he had earlier purchased access codes to the IOI network that could only be used by someone inside the IOI intranet since this cannot be accessed through the OASIS. Since becoming an IOI employee is (for various reasons) out of the question, Wade has become an IOI indentured servant. Once into the IOI system, Wade engages in some creative hacking and reprogramming.

Wade manages to download lots of data on IOI's attempts to enter the Third Gate. He also learns that IOI has been tracking himself, Art3mis, Aech, Shoto (with varying success) and video evidence showing IOI agents murdering Daito. Since IOI plans to abduct Aech and Shoto and has flagged them all "'to be disposed of'" later (293), Wade realizes he must break out of IOI sooner than he planned to save their lives.

One other discovery is a photograph of Art3mis (Samantha Evelyn Cook) showing a girl with a "reddish-purple birthmark" on the left half of her face (291). This explains why Art3mis has not wanted to meet Wade: she is embarrassed by her physical deformity. (We remember that Wade's own avatar shows him to be slimmer and with less acne than his real self.) For Wade, however, the birth-mark does not at all detract from the young woman's beauty. He reflects, "If anything, the face I saw in the photo seemed even more beautiful to me than that of her avatar, because I knew this one was real" (292). This is a huge moment of maturity for Wade.

0031

Question

38. In this chapter, Wade goes on the offensive. How does he manage to cover his tracks so that IOI cannot locate him?

Commentary

Frankly, it all seems a bit too easy for Wade in this chapter. The fact is that the author needs to get Wade reunited with the three remaining gunters as soon as possible – remember that IOI is actually at Castle Anorak and they only have to figure out how to open the Third Gate and it is 'Game Over'! For a society that seems to be falling apart, there seem to be lots of businesses selling high-end goods and Wade has no problems at all walking the city streets.

0032

Question

39. How and where has the reader been prepared for the sudden intervention of Ogden Morrow's avatar?

Commentary

Art3mis is angry that Wade accessed her file, despite the fact that, as Aech points out, Wade's action saved her life. Art3mis is annoyed that Wade has seen the birth mark on her face because she cannot believe that he will still find her attractive.

Wade explains that the Sixers are held up at the third gate because it is not in their nature to think of cooperation. He is sure that Halliday "'wanted to force us to work together,'" though the others are skeptical (308). Wade outlines his plan (though he does not say how the Sixers' shield around the castle is going to fall), but it has one massive flaw: each of the four major characters is homeless, on the run for their lives, and thus unable to get the kind of secure connection to the OASIS necessary for the operation. At that moment, Ogden Morrow's avatar appears.

The technical term for a narrative device such as this is deus ex machina which is defined by Merriam-Webster as "a person or thing (as in fiction or drama) that appears or is introduced suddenly and unexpectedly and provides a contrived solution to an apparently insoluble difficulty." An example would be the ending of William Golding's *The Lord of the Flies* when the boys, who seem about to plunge into total savagery, are suddenly rescued by a passing British Navy ship – an outside force whose arbitrary appearance resolves the plot. Of course, deus ex machina can be unconvincing and contrived, but in this case the reader really should have known that Ogden has been involved in the Hunt from the very start because the narrator has sprinkled clues throughout the story – most obviously the pile of magazines that the clumsy Og knocked over.

0033

Question

40. Were you surprised by Ache's identity? Do you find the revelation effective? Why? or Why not?

Commentary

Occasionally this commentary has suggested certain inconsistencies and improbabilities in the action, and the reader may have noticed some for him/herself. Here we come across a few more. First, being one of the co-creators of OASIS, Og seems to have effectively unlimited virtual powers. This was seen when he blasted all the Sixers who invaded his party at the nightclub. Why then does he not step in and end this thing? Why take the risk of IOI gaining Halliday's fortune and control of the OASIS? The Sixers have cheated and killed, so surely he should follow Halliday's instructions "'intervene if it became necessary'" (314). Second, in a world in economic collapse with an enduring energy crisis, airplanes seem to keep flying and airports stay open. Third, in a world where the countryside is a lawless place (remember the description of the armored bus on which Wade travelled between cities), Aech, who turns out to be a black female, seems to drive her electric RV about the country in complete safety. Each individual reader will decide whether these (and other) examples really *are* inconsistencies and the extent to which they detract from the story.

As the identities of the High Four (once the High Fives) are revealed, the author makes more than a nod towards multiculturalism and feminism. We have two Caucasians, one Japanese, and one African-American; we have two males and two females, one of whom is gay; we even have one person who considers her face to be scarred. In fact, in real life, none of the Four is particularly good looking. The novel seems to have a clear message that it is not the outside appearance of people that matters but their character and loyalty. Wade puts this idea into words when he reflects on his relationship with Aech, "We'd connected on a purely mental level. I understood her, trusted her, and loved her as a dear friend. None of that had changed, or could be changed by anything as inconsequential as her gender, or skin color, or sexual orientation" (321).

Og's intervention "'to maintain the integrity of Jim's game'" takes the form of offering the four gunters a safe place to live and access to state of the art Oasis equipment (315). This provides the narrative basis for the final confrontation, what Og calls "'the most epic battle in videogame history'" (325).

0034

Question

41. How has Wade programmed the destruction of the Sixer shield?

Commentary

How effectively can words portray the three dimensional, shape changing world of the OASIS, and more specifically of the biggest gathering of avatars for the biggest fight in the history of OASIS? Each reader will decide this for him/herself. The climax of the novel is certainly action-packed and exciting.

0035

Question

42. Explain why Halliday designed the Third Gate so that it could only be opened by three keys.

Commentary

Both Shoto and Wade are determined to kill Sorrento's avatar. Shoto says,

"'I owe this son of a bitch some payback,'" as though he feels that killing an avatar will be some measure of revenge for his brother's murder (338). Wade is more realistic since he knows that as soon as he kills Sorrento's avatar, Sorrento will be "kicking one of his underlings out of a haptic chair so he could take control of a new avatar" – one of the many ways in which the Sixers break the rules of the Hunt (341). Therefore, Wade's revenge takes the form of publically humiliating Sorrento. Wade comments, "He deserved to have his ass kicked while the whole world watched" (339).

The chapter ends with another tremendous 'hook': in the moment of triumph, Wade, Aech and Art3mis all die – or at least their avatars do. It is by no means clear to the reader what this means for the Hunt.

0036

Questions

43. How do you react to Wade's declaration that he is "'going to split the prize money" with Art3mis, Aech and Shoto whether they help him to get through the Third Gate or not?

Commentary

More deus ex machina here. First, Wade is the very first person in the entire history of the OASIS whose avatar gets a second life because of the mysterious quarter that he won for playing a perfect game of Pac-Man on Archaide which turns out to be "a single-use artifact that gave [his] avatar an extra life" (345). Wade admits that he had pretty much forgotten about having placed it in his inventory – and the author is betting that the reader has too. Second, Wade had lost all of his other artifacts and so is unable to get to the Third Gate which is hovering in midair until he finds Art3mis's "Black Chuck Taylor All Stars [sneakers which] … bestow their wearer with both speed and flight" (348). Conveniently, they seem to fit Wade perfectly.

More seriously, Wade has learned the importance of shared achievements and rewards. As he tells the others, he "'never would have gotten this far on [his] own,'" so he intends to share the prize with them whether they help him further of not (348-349).

0037

Question

44. How does the author make it clear that Wade's success is a group effort not an individual triumph?

Commentary

In playing the game *Tempest* Wade benefits from Art3mis's knowledge that the original game had "'a bug in the game code … [so that] if you died with a certain score, the machine would give you a bunch of free credits'" (351). This is the only way Wade could have bettered Halliday's score since, as he admits,

Tempest is not his best game. The Flicksync challenge is easier for Wade since he has seen the movie *Monty Python and the Holy Grail* "exactly 157 times … [and] knew every word by heart" (356). Nevertheless, at key moments the others are able to prompt him.

0038

Question

45. Explain what Halliday came to understand about OASIS near the end of his life.

Commentary

Once in the recreation of Halliday's office, Wade is alone. He works out that the password he needs is Leucosia which was the name of Kira's avatar. He remembers from Ogden Morrow's biography that only in the virtual world of the OASIS could Halliday speak to Kira "*in a relaxed manner … only in the character, as Anorak, during the course of our gaming sessions, and he would only address her as Leucosia, the name of her D&D character*" (361). This is a reminder that Halliday was never able to function in the real world.

When Wade finally meets Halliday's avatar, it is clear that, once he knew that he was dying, Halliday realized fully that he had never lived. He tells Wade, "'I created the OASIS because I never felt at home in the real world. I was afraid, for all my life. Right up until I knew it was ending. That was when I realized, as terrifying and as painful as reality can be, it's also the only place where you can find true happiness. Because reality is *real*'" (364). Of course, Wade understands this perfectly because he has had the same thought many times throughout the story. As if to reinforce the truth of this, Wade soon learns from the newsfeeds that Sorrento has been arrested.

0039

Question

46. How does the ending work for you? How effectively does it bring together the themes of the story?

Commentary

The final chapter is full of symbolism. Wade must solve the puzzle of a maze in order to find Art3mis, but it is "'an easy maze'" Og tells him (369), because it is a "identical to the labyrinth in Adventure" (370). The maze represents the OASIS through which Wade has navigated to meet the real Art3mis. When he sees her, the girl who has been worried about her disfiguring birthmark "had her hair brushed back, so [he] could see it" (370). It seems that she too is ready to function in the real world. When the two kiss, the sensation is better than anything in the virtual world. No wonder Wade ends, "It occurred to me that for the first time in as long as I could remember, I had absolutely no desire to long back into the OASIS" (372).

Thus, the final chapter hits all the right notes, but a lot is left unsaid. Aech and Shoto are the peripheral characters they have actually always been. The fate of OASIS is uncertain now that Wade had the capacity to hit the Big Red Button. Moreover, the fate of the world hangs in the balance. One doubts that even Halliday's vast fortune (split four ways) will be enough to end world hunger and poverty.

Perspectives

Below are a number of strongly expressed verdicts on the novel. Each could form the basis for group discussion or for a written response.

[T]he breadth and cleverness of Mr. Cline's imagination gets this daydream pretty far. But there comes a point when it is clear that Wade lacks at least one dimension and that gaming has overwhelmed everything else about this book. ("A Future Wrapped in 1980s Culture" by Janet Maslin, *The New York Times*, August 14, 2011)

So what's to like about the book? Everything! Ready Player One is not just homage to all things 80s pop culture: the movies, the music and, of course, classic arcade and roleplaying games, it's an addictive read so potent it can only be described as literary cocaine. The story grips hold of the reader and drags them through a dizzying adventure and when it finally ends, you feel light headed and disorientated. It's unputdownable! ("Ready Player One by Ernest Cline, A Recommended Book of the Month, *Fantasy Book Review*, Abbas Daya)

Ready Player One is written with such a depth of love for its subject that it reads like a digital historical novel … There is nothing in this book that I would change. The characters are believable teenagers with enough street cred to make them instantly viable in the real world. There is action on every page without it ever being overdone. ("Ready Player One by Ernest Cline, A Recommended Book of the Month, *Fantasy Book Review*, Matthew Bridle)

Set in 2044, that first sci-fi adventure took place in a dystopian future in which people escape their lives by jacking into a virtual reality universe. This VR world was created by a programmer who was obsessed with '80s geek culture and built an elaborate treasure hunt into the game based on his very specific predilections … Although this sounds like fertile ground for a critique of the inward-facing tendencies that so often pervade modern gaming, *Ready Player One* was far too joyously self-absorbed in its referential excesses to step back and examine what they might mean. It was still a page-turner, though. ("Serious Bill-Paying Skillage" by Laura Hudson, *The Slate Book Review*, July 7, 2015)

This escapist romp … immediately struck a chord with nerds – and wannabes – everywhere. ("Ready Player One: 80s-obsessed, focus of Oct.'s FDL Reads," *USA Today*, October 1, 2014)

I felt I was sort of battling through a lot of crap to get to the good stuff. For every awesome pop reference, there was the huge amount of exposition; for every cool mystery, there was the pedestrian writing; for every plot twist, a Deus Ex Machina; until eventually the fun times were completely eclipsed by the realisation [sic.] that this book might be *fun* but it is most certainly not good. Not in the opinion of this reader anyway. ("Joint Review: *Ready Player One* by Ernest Cline," Ana, *The Book Smugglers*, August 16, 2011)

[T]his is my main problem with this novel, that it brings up really important and complicated issues then brushes them aside simplistically. You can include there not only the gender and race issues but also the stuff happening in the real world: the poverty, the wars, the energy crisis, the murders. ("Joint Review: *Ready Player One* by Ernest Cline," Ana, *The Book Smugglers*, August 16, 2011)

The tension between the Sixers (those GSS employees hellbent on discovering Halliday's egg and winning absolute control of OASIS) and gunters (true believers that hunt for the egg to uphold the ideals of opensource geekdom, man) is beautifully rendered and fraught with serious tension. ("Joint Review: *Ready Player One* by Ernest Cline," Thea, *The Book Smugglers*, August 16, 2011)

[After the failed attempt to kill him] Parzival threads his way between more '80s games and movies to gain the other keys; it's clever but not exciting. Even a romance with another avatar and the ultimate "epic throwdown" fail to stir the blood. Too much puzzle-solving, not enough suspense. (Kirkus Review, May 1, 2011)

It should be noted that Cline's talent shines through when he's working in his comfort zone. The author has a sincere love for every game and movie he squishes into the pages of *Ready Player One*, and the quest for Halliday's egg is at times clever and thrilling. However, by the end of the novel, we're left with an experience as hollow and manufactured as the virtual world of the OASIS. (John Jarzemsky, "Ready Player One" by Ernest Cline, *Lit Reactor* Review, November 9, 2011)

Literary terms activity

As you use each term in the study guide, fill in the definition of the term and include an example from the text to show how it is used. The first definition is supplied. Find an example in the text to complete it.

Term	Definition
	Example
Ambiguous, ambiguity	*When a statement is unclear in meaning- ambiguity may be deliberate or accidental*
Antagonist	
Deus ex machina	
Diction	
Foreshadowing	
Hyperbole	

Term	Definition
	Example
Infer/inference	
Irony/ironic	
Dramatic irony	
Metaphor/ metaphorical	
Extended metaphor	
Motivation/ motive	

Ready Player One by Ernest Cline

Term	Definition
	Example
Narrative voice	
Role	
Sarcasm	
Simile	
Extended simile	
Suspense	

Term	Definition
	Example
Symbol/ symbolic/ symbolism/ symbolize	
Themes	
Tone	

Literary terms

Allegorical: a story in which the characters, their actions and the settings represent abstract ideas (often moral ideas) or historical/political events.

Ambiguous, ambiguity: when a statement is unclear in meaning – ambiguity may be deliberate or accidental.

Analogy: a comparison which treats two things as identical in one or more specified ways.

Antagonist: a character or force opposing the protagonist.

Antithesis: the complete opposite of something.

Authorial comment: when the writer addresses the reader directly (not to be confused with the narrator doing so).

Climax: the conflict to which the action has been building since the start of the play or story.

Colloquialism: the casual, informal mainly spoken language of ordinary people – often called "slang."

Comic hyperbole: deliberately inflated, extravagant language used for comic effect.

Comic Inversion: reversing the normally accepted order of things for comic effect.

Connotation: the ideas, feelings and associations generated by a word or phrase.

Dark comedy: comedy which has a serious implication – comedy that deals with subjects not usually treated humorously (e.g., death).

Deus ex machina: an unnatural or very unlikely turn of events in a story that resolves or removes one or more problems faced by a character or characters.

Dialogue: a conversation between two or more people in direct speech.

Diction: the writer's choice of words in order to create a particular effect.

Equivocation: saying something which is capable of two interpretations with the intention of misrepresenting the truth.

Euphemism: a polite word for an ugly truth – for example, a person is said to be sleeping when they are actually dead.

Fallacy: a misconception resulting from incorrect reasoning.

First person: first person singular is "I" and plural is "we".

Foreshadow: a statement or action which gives the reader a hint of what is likely to happen later in the narrative.

Form of speech: the register in which speech is written – the diction reflects the character.

Frame narrative: a story within which the main narrative is placed.

Genre: the type of literature into which a particular text falls (e.g. drama, poetry, novel).

Hubris: pride – in Greek tragedy it is the hero's belief that he can challenge the will of the gods.

Hyperbole: exaggeration designed to create a particular effect.

Image, imagery: figurative language such as simile, metaphor, personification etc., or a description which conjures up a particularly vivid picture.

Imply, implication: when the text suggests to the reader a meaning which it does not actually state.

Infer, inference: the reader's act of going beyond what is stated in the text to draw conclusions.

Irony, ironic: a form of humor which undercuts the apparent meaning of a statement:

> *Conscious irony:* irony used deliberately by a writer or character;
>
> *Unconscious irony:* a statement or action which has significance for the reader of which the character is unaware;
>
> *Dramatic irony*: when an action has an important significance that is obvious to the reader but not to one or more of the characters;
>
> *Tragic irony:* when a character says (or does) something which will have a serious, even fatal, consequence for him/ her. The audience is aware of the error, but the character is not;
>
> *Verbal irony*: the conscious use of particular words which are appropriate to what is being said.

Juxtaposition: literally putting two things side by side for purposes of comparison and/ or contrast.

Literal: the surface level of meaning that a statement has.

Melodramatic: action and/or dialogue that is inflated or extravagant – frequently used for comic effect.

Metaphor, metaphorical: the description of one thing by direct comparison with another (e.g. the coal-black night).

Extended metaphor: a comparison which is developed at length.

Microcosm: literally 'the world is little' – a situation which reflects truths about the world in general.

Mood: the feelings and emotions contained in and/ or produced by a work of art (text, painting, music, etc.).

Motif: a frequently repeated idea, image or situation in a text.

Motivation: why a character acts as he/she does – in modern literature motivation is seen as psychological.

Narrator: the voice that the reader hears in the text – not to be confused with the author.

Frame narrative /story: a story within which the main story is told (e.g. *Heart of Darkness* by Conrad begins with five men on a boat in the Thames and then one of them tells the story of his experiences on the river Congo).

Oxymoron: the juxtaposition of two terms normally thought of as opposite (e.g. the silent scream).

Parable: a story with a moral lesson (e.g. the Good Samaritan).

Paradox, paradoxical: a statement or situation which appears self-contradictory and therefore absurd.

Pathos: is pity, or rather the ability of a text to make the audience or reader feel pity.

Perspective: point of view from which a story, or an incident within a story, is told.

Personified, personification: a simile or metaphor in which an inanimate object or abstract idea is described by comparison with a human.

Plot: a chain of events linked by cause and effect.

Prologue: an introduction which gives a lead-in to the main story.

Protagonist: the character who initiates the action and is most likely to have the sympathy of the audience.

Pun: a deliberate play on words where a particular word has two or more meanings both appropriate in some way to what is being said.

Realism: a text that describes the action in a way that appears to reflect life.

Rhetoric: any use of language designed to make the expression of ideas more effective (e.g. repetition, imagery, alliteration, etc.).

Sarcasm: stronger than irony – it involves a deliberate attack on a person or idea with the intention of mocking.

Satire, Satiric: the use of comedy to criticize attack, belittle, or humiliate – more extreme than irony.

Setting: the environment in which the narrative (or part of the narrative) takes place.

Simile: a description of one thing by explicit comparison with another (e.g. my love is like a red, red rose).

    Extended simile: a comparison which is developed at length.

Style: the way in which a writer chooses to express him/ herself. Style is a vital aspect of meaning since how something is expressed can crucially affect what is being written or spoken.

Suspense: the building of tension in the reader.

Symbol, symbolic, symbolism, symbolize: a physical object which comes to represent an abstract idea (e.g. the sun may symbolize life).

Themes: important concepts, beliefs and ideas explored and presented in a text.

Third person: third person singular is "he/ she/ it" and plural is "they" – authors often write novels in the third person.

Tone: literally the sound of a text – How words sound (either in the mouth of an actor or the head of a reader) can crucially affect meaning/

Tragic: King Richard III and Macbeth are both murderous tyrants, yet only Macbeth is a *tragic* figure. Why? Because Macbeth has the potential to be great, recognizes the error he has made and all that he has lost in making it, and dies bravely in a way that seems to accept the justice of the punishment.

Graphic Organizer- plot

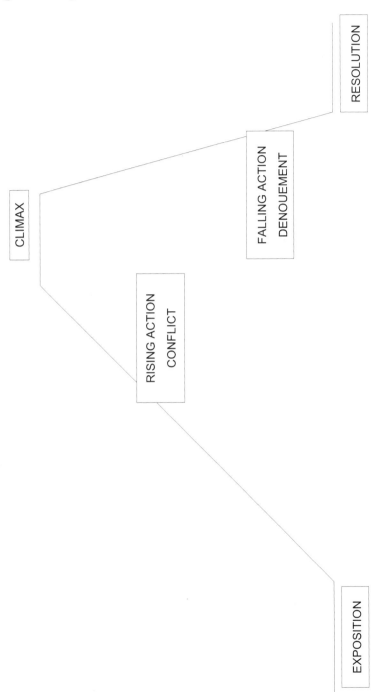

Graphic Organizer- perspectives

Different perspectives on the situation which initiates the action in the novel

Art3mis

Wade

Aech

Sorrento

The real world versus the virtual world of the OASIS

Reading Group Use of the Study Guide Questions

Although there are both closed and open questions in the Study Guide, very few of them have simple, right or wrong answers. They are designed to encourage in-depth discussion, disagreement, and (eventually) consensus. Above all, they aim to encourage readers to go to the text to support their conclusions and interpretations.

I am not so arrogant as to presume to tell readers how they should use this resource. I used it in the following ways, each of which ensured that group members were well prepared for group discussion and presentations.

1. Set a reading assignment for the group and tell everyone to be aware that the questions will be the focus of whole group discussion at the next meeting.

2. Set a reading assignment for the group and allocate particular questions to sections of the group (e.g. if there are four questions, divide the group into four sections, etc.).
In the meeting, form discussion groups containing one person who has prepared each question and allow time for feedback within the groups.
Have feedback to the whole the on each question by picking a group at random to present their answers and to follow up with a group discussion.

3. Set a reading assignment for the group, but do not allocate questions.
In the meeting, divide readers into groups and allocate to each group one of the questions related to the reading assignment, the answer to which they will have to present formally to the meeting.
Allow time for discussion and preparation.

4. Set a reading assignment for the group, but do not allocate questions.
In the meeting, divide readers into groups and allocate to each group one of the questions related to the reading assignment.
Allow time for discussion and preparation.
Now reconfigure the groups so that each group contains at least one person who has prepared each question and allow time for feedback within the groups.

5. Before starting to read the text, allocate specific questions to individuals or pairs. (It is best not to allocate all questions to allow for other approaches and variety. One in three questions or one in four seems about right.) Tell readers that they will be leading the group discussion on their question. They will need to start with a brief presentation of the issues and then conduct a question and answer session. After this, they will be expected to present a brief review of the discussion.

6. Having finished the text, arrange the meeting into groups of 3, 4 or 5. Tell each group to select as many questions from the Study Guide as there are members of the group.
Each individual is responsible for drafting out an answer to one question, and each answer should be substantial.
Each group as a whole is then responsible for discussing, editing and suggesting improvements to each answer.

To the Reader,

Ray strives to make his products the best that they can be. If you have any comments or questions about this book *please* contact the author through his email: **moore.ray1@yahoo.com**

Visit his website at **http://www.raymooreauthor.com**

Also by Ray Moore: Most books are available from amazon.com as paperbacks and at most online eBook retailers.

Fiction:

The Lyle Thorne Mysteries: each book features five tales from the Golden Age of Detection:

Investigations of The Reverend Lyle Thorne
Further Investigations of The Reverend Lyle Thorne
Early Investigations of Lyle Thorne
Sanditon Investigations of The Reverend Lyle Thorne
Final Investigations of The Reverend Lyle Thorne
Lost Investigations of The Reverend Lyle Thorne

Non-fiction:

The *Critical Introduction series* is written for high school teachers and students and for college undergraduates. Each volume gives an in-depth analysis of a key text:

"The General Prologue" by Geoffrey Chaucer: A Critical Introduction
"The Great Gatsby" by F. Scott Fitzgerald: A Critical Introduction
"Pride and Prejudice" by Jane Austen: A Critical Introduction
"The Stranger" by Albert Camus: A Critical Introduction (Revised Second Edition)

The *Text and Critical Introduction series* differs from the Critical introduction series as these books contain the original text and in the case of the medieval texts an interlinear translation to aid the understanding of the text. The commentary allows the reader to develop a deeper understanding of the text and themes within the text.

"Sir Gawain and the Green Knight": Text and Critical Introduction
"The General Prologue" by Geoffrey Chaucer: Text and Critical Introduction
"Heart of Darkness" by Joseph Conrad: Text and Critical Introduction
"Henry V" by William Shakespeare: Text and Critical Introduction
"Oedipus Rex" by Sophocles: Text and Critical Introduction

"A Room with a View" By E.M. Forster: Text and Critical Introduction
"The Sign of Four" by Sir Arthur Conan Doyle Text and Critical Introduction
"The Wife of Bath's Prologue and Tale" by Geoffrey Chaucer: Text and Critical Introduction

Study guides available in print - listed alphabetically by author

* denotes also available as an eBook

"ME and EARL and the Dying GIRL" by Jesse Andrews: A Study Guide
"Pride and Prejudice" by Jane Austen: A Study Guide
"Moloka'i" by Alan Brennert: A Study Guide
"Wuthering Heights" by Emily Brontë: A Study Guide *
"Jane Eyre" by Charlotte Brontë: A Study Guide *
"The Stranger" by Albert Camus: A Study Guide
"The Myth of Sisyphus" and "The Stranger" by Albert Camus: Two Study Guides *
"The Awakening" by Kate Chopin: A Study Guide
Study Guide on Seven Short Stories by Kate Chopin
Study Guide on "Disgrace" by J. M. Coetzee
"The Meursault Investigation" by Kamel Daoud: A Study Guide
"Great Expectations" by Charles Dickens: A Study Guide *
"The Sign of Four" by Sir Arthur Conan Doyle: A Study Guide *
"The Wasteland, Prufrock and Poems" by T.S. Eliot: A Study Guide
"The Great Gatsby" by F. Scott Fitzgerald: A Study Guide
"A Room with a View" by E. M. Forster: A Study Guide
"Looking for Alaska" by John Green: A Study Guide
"Paper Towns" by John Green: A Study Guide
"Catch-22" by Joseph Heller: A Study Guide *
"Unbroken" by Laura Hillenbrand: A Study Guide
"The Kite Runner" by Khaled Hosseini: A Study Guide
"A Thousand Splendid Suns" by Khaled Hosseini: A Study Guide
"The Secret Life of Bees" by Sue Monk Kidd: A Study Guide
"Go Set a Watchman" by Harper Lee: A Study Guide
"On the Road" by Jack Keruoac: A Study Guide
"Life of Pi" by Yann Martel: A Study Guide *
Study Guide on "The Bluest Eye" by Toni Morrison
"Animal Farm" by George Orwell: A Study Guide
Study Guide on "Nineteen Eighty-Four" by George Orwell

Study Guide on "Selected Poems" and Additional Poems by Sylvia Plath*
"An Inspector Calls" by J.B. Priestley: A Study Guide
"Esperanza Rising" by Pam Munoz Ryan: A Study Guide
"The Catcher in the Rye" by J.D. Salinger: A Study Guide
"Where'd You Go, Bernadette" by Maria Semple: A Study Guide
"Henry V" by William Shakespeare: A Study Guide
Study Guide on "Macbeth" by William Shakespeare *
"Othello" by William Shakespeare: A Study Guide *
"Cannery Row" by John Steinbeck: A Study Guide
"East of Eden" by John Steinbeck: A Study Guide
"The Grapes of Wrath" by John Steinbeck: A Study Guide
"Of Mice and Men" by John Steinbeck: A Study Guide*
"Antigone" by Sophocles: A Study Guide *
"Oedipus Rex" by Sophocles: A Study Guide
"The Goldfinch" by Donna Tartt: A Study Guide
"Walden; or, Life in the Woods" by Henry David Thoreau: A Study Guide
Study Guide on "Cat's Cradle" by Kurt Vonnegut
"The Bridge of San Luis Rey" by Thornton Wilder: A Study Guide *
Study Guide on "The Book Thief" by Markus Zusak

Study Guides available as e-books:
A Study Guide on "Heart of Darkness" by Joseph Conrad
A Study Guide on "The Mill on the Floss" by George Eliot
A Study Guide on "Lord of the Flies" by William Golding
A Study Guide on "Nineteen Eighty-Four" by George Orwell
A Study Guide on "Henry IV Part 2" by William Shakespeare
A Study Guide on "Julius Caesar" by William Shakespeare
A Study Guide on "The Pearl" by John Steinbeck
A Study Guide on "Slaughterhouse-Five" by Kurt Vonnegut
New titles are added regularly.

Teacher resources:

Ray also publishes many more study guides and other resources for classroom use on the 'Teachers Pay Teachers' website:
http://www.teacherspayteachers.com/Store/Raymond-Moore

EXPRESS

ALLSTATE

PREMIER

POWERDE

~~scribble~~

ROSSTATE

CHEST

TOMMY

NOLA

CHARLESTON

BEACH

TAPES 7 DIGITAL

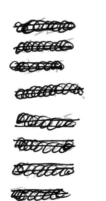